NATIONAL GEOGRAPHIC
KiDS

weird but true!

1

350 OUTRAGEOUS FACTS

NATIONAL GEOGRAPHIC
WASHINGTON, D.C.

4

Cheetahs can change direction in midair when chasing prey.

A SHEEP, A DUCK, AND A ROOSTER WERE THE FIRST PASSENGERS ON A HOT-AIR BALLOON.

BAA.

COCK-A-DOODLE-DOO.

QUACK.

Google.com is named after the number googol—

10000000000000000000
00000000000000000000
00000000000000000000

Tia the Neapolitan mastiff gave birth to **24 puppies** in one litter.

Girls have more taste buds than boys do.

a one followed by a hundred zeros.

OOOOOOOOOOOOOOOOOOOOOOO
OOOOOOOOOOOOOOOOOOOOOOO
OOOOOOOOOOOOOOOOOOOOOO

The
tallest
known
snowman
was
higher than
a 12-story
building.

SOME HONEYBEE QUEENS QUACK.

A bat can eat 3,000 insects in one night.

The most overdue library book was 288 years late.

The
world's largest
yo-yo
is nearly
12 feet (3.7 m) tall and weighs about as much as **three** polar bears.

***Star Wars* creators designed Yoda to look like Albert Einstein.**

IN JAPAN, THERE ARE WATERMELONS SHAPED LIKE PYRAMIDS.

167 letters

Krungthep
Ratanakosin Mahinthar
Mahadilokpop Nopar
Udomratchanivet Maha
Avatarnsathit Sakkath
officially known as

are in the world's longest place-name, Mahanakhon Bovorn ayutthaya atratchathani Burirom sathan Amornpiman attiyavisnukarmprasit, **Bangkok, Thailand.**

New York City's Empire State Building was built with **ten million** bricks.

A coffin was once designed to look like a **lobster.**

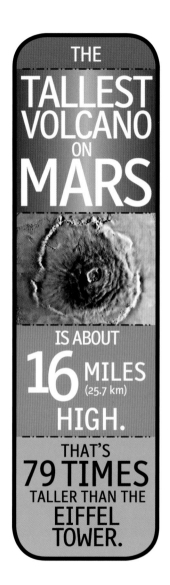

THE **TALLEST** VOLCANO ON **MARS**

IS ABOUT **16** MILES (25.7 km) **HIGH.**

THAT'S **79 TIMES** TALLER THAN THE **EIFFEL TOWER.**

PEANUT
BUTTER
CAN BE
CONVERTED INTO A
DIAMOND.

If you could travel the speed of light, you would never get older.

BELLY BUTTON LINT

IS MADE OF CLOTHING FIBERS, HAIR, AND DEAD SKIN CELLS.

THE OLDEST CONTINUOUSLY STANDING TREE ON EARTH IS NEARLY 5,000 YEARS OLD— ABOUT THE SAME AGE AS THE PYRAMIDS OF EGYPT.

19

A woman hand-delivered a pizza

from London, England, to Melbourne, Australia—

a distance of about 10,350 miles.

(16,657 km)

Your **FINGERNAILS** take six months to grow from base to tip.

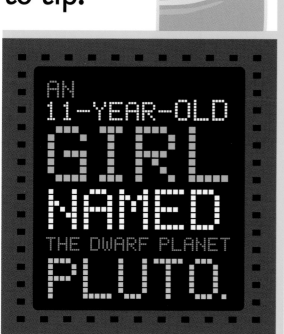

AN
11-YEAR-OLD
GIRL
NAMED
THE DWARF PLANET
PLUTO.

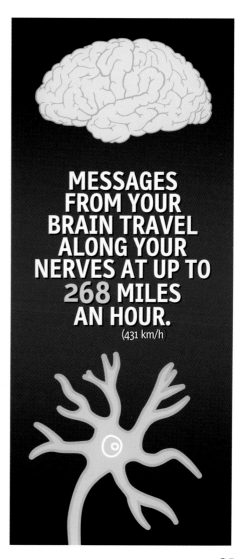

MESSAGES FROM YOUR BRAIN TRAVEL ALONG YOUR NERVES AT UP TO **268** MILES AN HOUR.
(431 km/h)

A SNEEZE TRAVELS 100 MILES AN HOUR. ^(161 km/h)

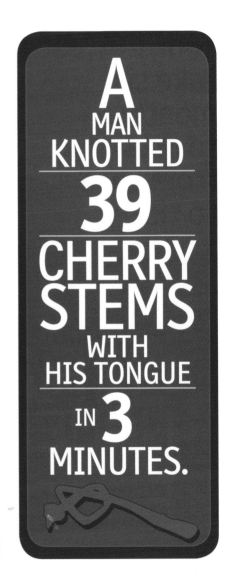

A MAN KNOTTED 39 CHERRY STEMS WITH HIS TONGUE IN 3 MINUTES.

The world's **biggest flower**—found in the Indonesian rain forest—can grow **wider than a car tire.**

THE FOUNDERS OF THE TOY COMPANY DOLLS AFTER THEIR

KEN AND BARB

MATTEL
NAMED TWO
CHILDREN:

IE.

THERE
ARE ABOUT A

BILLION
BACTERIA

IN YOUR MOUTH
RIGHT NOW.

Cockroaches can survive **underwater** for up to **15 minutes.**

The first bubble gum, made in 1906, was called Blibber-Blubber.

ABOUT TEN THOUSAND OF THE CELLS IN YOUR BODY COULD FIT ON THE HEAD OF A PIN.

Applesauce
was the first food
eaten in space
by an American astronaut.

Phasmophobia is the fear of ghosts.

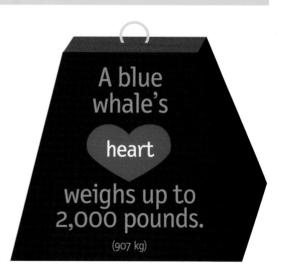

A blue whale's **heart** weighs up to 2,000 pounds.

(907 kg)

Slugs have 3,000 teeth

and 4 noses.

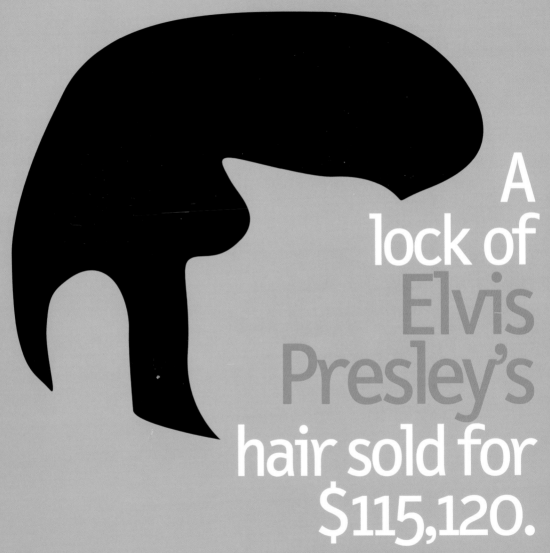

A
lock of
Elvis
Presley's
hair sold for
$115,120.

SOME CARS
CAN RUN ON
USED FRENCH-
FRY OIL.

HOT DOGS

CAN LAST MORE THAN 20 YEARS

IN LANDFILLS.

The eastern spotted **skunk** does a handstand before it **sprays.**

About a million Earths could fit inside the sun.

THE BRIGHTEST LIGHT ON A HOTEL—IN LAS VEGAS, NEVADA, IN THE UNITED STATES— CAN BE SEEN FROM AIRPLANES 250 MILES AWAY. (402 km)

THE PROTOTYPE OF THE ORIGINAL G.I. JOE DOLL SOLD FOR $200,000.

Almost **90%** of **snow** is **air.**

HONEY
NEVER
SPOILS.

ONE OF THE WORLD'S LIGHTEST MAMMALS
—THE BUMBLEBEE BAT—
WEIGHS ABOUT AS MUCH AS TWO M&M'S.

MOTHS CAN SMELL EACH OTHER FROM MILES {km} AWAY.

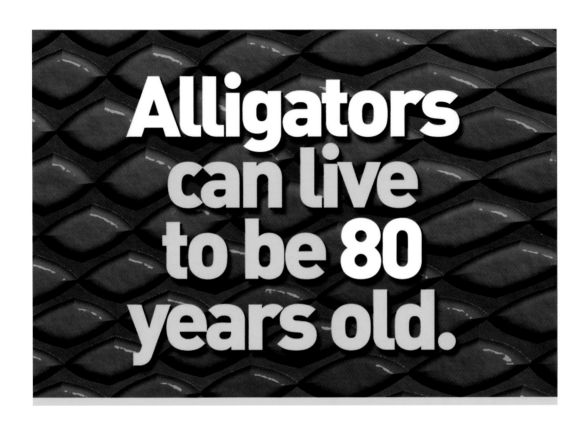

Alligators can live to be 80 years old.

A large python can swall

Bats
are the only
mammals
that fly.

SOME SNAILS CAN SLEEP FOR THREE YEARS.

ow a goat whole.

SOME FROGS CAN GLIDE UP TO 50 FEET (15 m) THROUGH THE AIR.

All the **CRAYOLA CRAYONS** made each year **would** circle the globe **SIX TIMES.**

Researchers are working to use **SPIDER SILK** to help **REPAIR HUMAN NERVES.**

People in **France** use **HEART EMOJIS** in their text messages **more than people in any other country,** according to a study.

A SCHOOL in northern Thailand has a **SPORTS ARENA MADE** entirely out **OF BAMBOO.** (It can fit 300 students!)

5,000-YEAR-OLD WATERMELON SEEDS were discovered at an archaeological site in Libya.

Every August, people in a Belgium town **COOK A GIANT OMELET** using about **10,000 EGGS.**

ALPACAS like to **SUNBATHE.**

HOLLYWOOD is the name of a cemetery in Richmond, Virginia, U.S.A.

AN ISLAND NEAR BRAZIL is home to so many **VENOMOUS VIPERS** that **people need permission to visit.**

That's Weird!

The **BIG BANG** was **SILENT.**

A POST OFFICE in Alma, Colorado, U.S.A., is **10,578 FEET** (3,224 m) **ABOVE SEA LEVEL—** as high as **8.5 EMPIRE STATE BUILDINGS.**

On average, **U.S. DOG OWNERS** GIVE THEIR PETS **FIVE** PRESENTS a year.

A beefalo is part bison, part cow.

A man **sculpted a statue** of himself using his own **hair, teeth, and nails.**

IF GRASSHOPPERS WERE THE SIZE OF PEOPLE, THEY COULD LEAP THE LENGTH OF A **BASKETBALL COURT.**

BOLTS OF LIGHTNING CAN SHOOT OUT OF AN ERUPTING VOLCANO.

HORSES RUN ON THEIR toes.

Dragonflies can see in all directions at once.

There
are

48

different
shades of
red Crayola
crayons.

brick red

magenta

red

violet red

red violet

wild strawbe

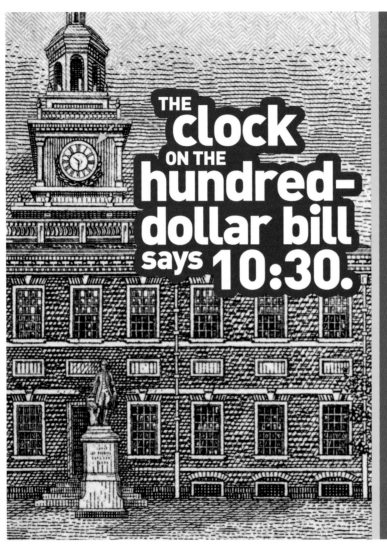

THE **clock** ON THE **hundred-dollar bill** says **10:30.**

WEDDING GOWNS HAVE BEEN MADE OUT OF TOILET PAPER.

SOME **FISH** CAN WALK ON LAND.

You can see a **1,700-pound** (771-kg) chocolate moose named **Lenny** in Maine, U.S.A.

Scuba **divers** send postcards from a mailbox off the coast of **Japan** that's nearly **33 feet** (10 m) underwater.

The **LARGEST** pumpkin pie **WEIGHED 3,699** pounds. (1,678 kg)

51

A camel doesn't **sweat** until its body temperature reaches **106°F.** (41°C)

Writers once used **bread crumbs** instead of **erasers** to correct pencil mistakes.

A waterfall in Hawaii sometimes goes up instead of down.

Cats

communicate using at least 16 known "cat words."

IT'S POSSIBLE FOR A SHARK TO DETECT A **FISH'S HEARTBEAT** BEFORE IT ATTACKS.

You can buy a piece of meteorite on eBay.

DOLPHINS CAN HEAR
SOUNDS
UNDERWATER FROM
15 MILES (24 km)
AWAY.

African elephants have ears shaped like the continent of Africa.

Porcupines CAN float.

58

An average yawn lasts about six seconds.

Koalas and **humans** have similar fingerprints.

Opposite sides of **dice** always add up to **7.**

IT'S ILLEGAL TO SELL A **HAUNTED HOUSE** IN NEW YORK **WITHOUT TELLING** THE BUYER.

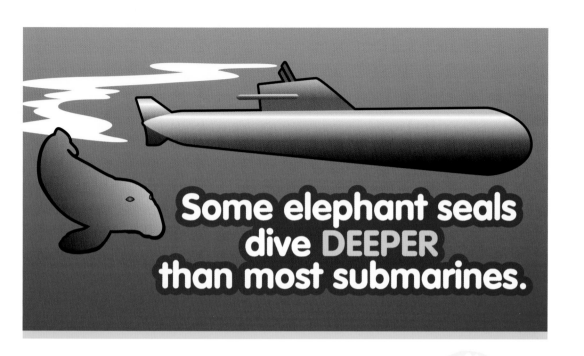

Some elephant seals dive DEEPER than most submarines.

It gets so cold **in Siberia** that your breath can turn to ice in midair.

A WEBSITE
SELLS LAND ON
MARS...

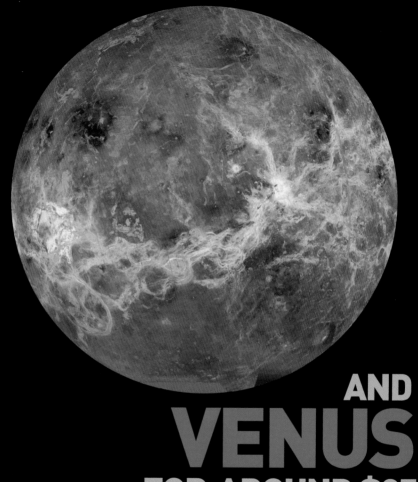

AND
VENUS
FOR AROUND $25
AN ACRE.
(0.4 ha)

ANTEATERS
don't have TEETH.

Hippo sweat is
red. 🔴

Some salamanders regrow their tails, legs, and even parts of their eyes.

A tiger's skin is  like its fur.

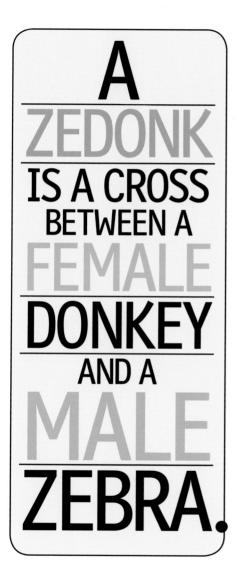

A
ZEDONK
IS A CROSS
BETWEEN A
FEMALE
DONKEY
AND A
MALE
ZEBRA.

Abracadabra
used to be written in a triangle
shape to keep away evil spirits.

ABRACADABRA
ABRACADABR
ABRACADAB
ABRACADA
ABRACAD
ABRACA
ABRAC
ABRA
ABR
AB
A

A **Slinky** can **stretch** from a sixth-floor window to the ground.

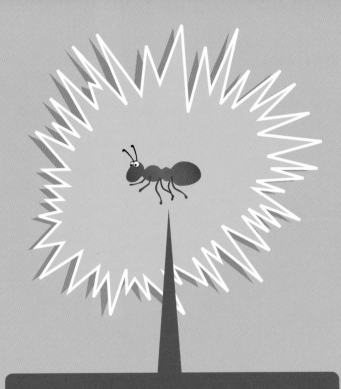

SOME ANTS MAKE THEMSELVES EXPLODE WHEN ATTACKED.

Chameleons change color in as few as 20 seconds.

A **battery** can be made out of a **potato.**

JELLYFISH STING EVEN WHEN DEAD.

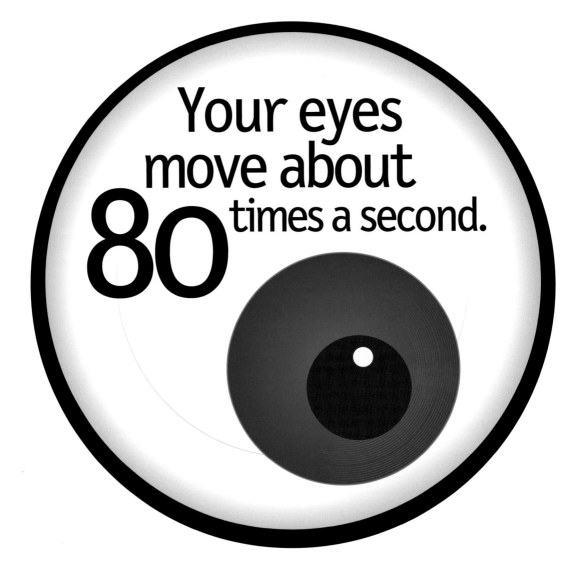

Your eyes move about 80 times a second.

A lobster's teeth are in its **stomach.**

A DOLPHIN CAN LEARN TO RECOGNIZE ITSELF IN THE **MIRROR.**

YOU CAN SEE AUTUMN LEAVES FROM SPACE.

74

There's a
**heart-
shaped
coral
reef**
in Australia.

At
least **124** rocks
from
Mars
have landed on
Earth.

A SLOTH WOULD TAKE A MONTH TO TRAVEL A SINGLE MILE.

(1.6 km)

A **U.S. dollar bill** can be folded in the same spot about **4,000 times** before it tears.

Chicks can **breathe** through their **shells.**

Pet hamsters **run** up to **eight miles** (13 km) a night on a **wheel.**

AN AVERAGE OF MORE THAN **1.2 MILLION PEOPLE** ARE **FLYING** OVERHEAD IN **AIRCRAFT** AT ANY GIVEN TIME.

New York

drifts about an inch (2.5 cm) farther from

London

every year.

In the open ocean, a **tsunami** sometimes travels as fast as a jet plane.

A mountain climber carried the **Olympic torch** to the top of **Mount Everest.**

Owls can't move their eyeballs.

From Earth you always look at the **same side** of the **moon.**

The biggest bald eagle nests weigh up to 4,000 pounds. (1,814 kg)

Kangaroos don't hop backward.

Thieves in Germany STOLE AS MUCH AS $82,000 WORTH OF SWEETS from a tractor trailer.

STUDENTS in the Netherlands have DESIGNED A BUS that runs on the same acid found in ant stings.

The **DEEPEST POINT** for **CAPTURING A FISH ON VIDEO** was **FIVE MILES** (8 km) **UNDER THE OCEAN'S SURFACE.**

The first modern **OLYMPIC SWIMMING COMPETITIONS** were held in the **MEDITERRANEAN SEA.**

A researcher **CREATED A BATTERY** using only paper and a bacteria-containing drop of liquid.

7,200 = approximate number of **BOOKS LEFT BEHIND** on **LONDON'S MASS TRANSIT SYSTEM** every year

A **VIRUS CAN TURN CATERPILLARS INTO "ZOMBIES,"** making them act against their will.

A woman in Pennsylvania, U.S.A., made a **DRESS** out of more than **10,000 CANDY WRAPPERS.**

84

If you **WEIGH** 100 POUNDS (45 kg) **on** EARTH, you'd **WEIGH** 253 POUNDS (115 kg) **on** JUPITER.

A man doing yard work in **New London, North Carolina, U.S.A.,** found a stash of weapons **THOUSANDS OF YEARS OLD.**

Nearly one-third **of the** U.S. states **begin with the** letters M or N.

That's Weird!

There is a **SECRET STAIRCASE** in New York City's **GRAND CENTRAL TERMINAL.**

ROCK HYRAXES, 10-pound (4.5-kg) animals that look like guinea pigs, are related to elephants and manatees.

It's possible for people to get

goose bumps

on their face.

Some **humming-birds** weigh less than a **penny.**

Tornadoes usually spin in opposite directions above and below the Equator.

It would take about **three years of nonstop pedaling to bike to the moon.**

Food passes through the

giant squid's

brain on the way to its **stomach.**

Clams can live to be more than a hundred years old.

WHO ARE YOU CALLING OLD?

The end of the minute hand on **London's Big Ben** clock travels about **118** miles (190 km) a year.

An avalanche can travel **80** MILES AN HOUR. (129 km/h)

Americans drive an average of more than **13,000 miles** (20,921 km) per year— more than half the circumference of Earth.

A church IN THE Czech Republic HAS A chandelier made of human bones.

97%
of Earth's water
is salt water.

Dust from Africa can travel all the way to Florida.

Humans can recognize about **10,000** different smells.

BUTTERFLIES taste food with their feet.

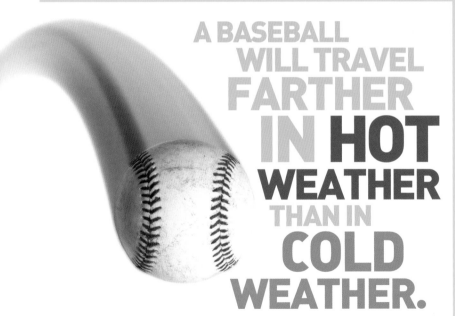

A BASEBALL WILL TRAVEL FARTHER IN HOT WEATHER THAN IN COLD WEATHER.

Snakes can't slither on glass.

A RESTAURANT OWNER MADE A **6,000-GALLON** (22,706 L) MILKSHAKE— ENOUGH TO FILL MORE THAN **100** BATHTUBS.

93

HIPPOS
can be
more
dangerous
than
LIONS.

The fastest falcon can outpace a speeding race car.

Kids BLINK about **five million** times a year.

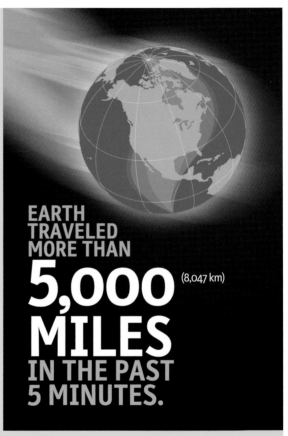

EARTH TRAVELED MORE THAN

5,000 (8,047 km)
MILES
IN THE PAST 5 MINUTES.

Bakers in Turkey made an 8,891-foot-long cake— (2,710-m) **that's the length of about 114 tennis courts!**

The Himalayan **mountains** grow a half inch taller each year. (1.3 cm)

IF ABOUT **33 MILLION PEOPLE** HELD HANDS, THEY COULD MAKE A CIRCLE AROUND THE EQUATOR.

97

Some ants can lift
50 TIMES
their own weight.
(That's like a kid carrying a car!)

In ancient Egypt, **mummies' brains** were removed through the **nose.**

THE AVERAGE **$100** BILL CIRCULATES FOR **15** YEARS.

FOUR-THOUSAND-YEAR-OLD NOODLES WERE DISCOVERED IN ANCIENT RUINS IN CHINA.

A HUNDRED-YEAR-OLD CHOCOLATE BAR SOLD FOR NEARLY $700.

THE MOST EXPENSIVE ITEM EVER SOLD ON eBay WAS A $168-MILLION YACHT.

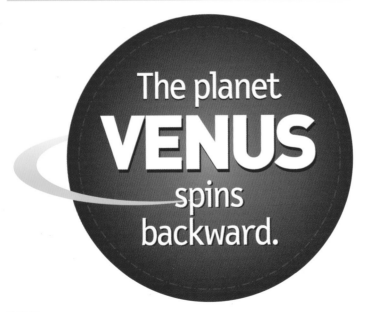

The planet **VENUS** spins backward.

IF YOU HEAT A DIAMOND TO 1405°F, (763°C) IT WILL TURN INTO VAPOR.

PEOPLE REPORT THE MOST UFO SIGHTINGS WHEN VENUS IS CLOSEST TO EARTH.

Australia was once a British prison colony.

The Asian vampire **moth** sometimes **drinks** the **blood** of animals.

A New York man did a continuous series of somersaults for 12 miles, **390 yards.**
(19 km)
(357 m)

A person once "hiccuped" for **68** years.

A clock runs faster on a tall mountain than at sea level.

Astronauts orbiting Earth see up to 16 sunrises and sunsets every day.

Many birds' **feathers** weigh more than their **bones.**

A caterpillar

has **more muscles** than a **human.**

You can *fry an egg* on a hot sidewalk

ICELAND DOESN'T ONLY HAVE EARTHQUAKES; IT ALSO HAS ICEQUAKES.

when it reaches 158°F. (70°C)

Chewing gum burns about **11** calories an hour.

YOUR EYES PROCESS MORE THAN **120** MILLION BITS OF INFORMATION EVERY SECOND.

Scientists discovered a PLANET that "SNOWS" SUNSCREEN.

A flea can jump 100 times its body length—that's like you jumping to the top of a 34-story building!

The color red doesn't really make **bulls angry;** they are **•color-blind.**

No one knows for sure what color dinosaurs were.

DAYS ARE LONGER THAN YEARS ON THE PLANET MERCURY.

THE FIRST CANDY CANES WERE MADE WITHOUT STRIPES.

Cat urine can glow under black light.

SOME FISH CHANGE FROM FEMALE TO MALE.

The average American eats enough hamburger meat in a lifetime to equal the weight of a family car.

IF EARTH DIDN'T TILT, WE WOULDN'T HAVE SEASONS.

OUR PLANET HAS THE SAME AMOUNT OF **WATER TODAY** AS IT DID **100 MILLION YEARS AGO.**

A sea turtle

can weigh as much as a water buffalo.

There are more **PLASTIC** **FLAMINGOS** IN THE U.S.A. than real ones.

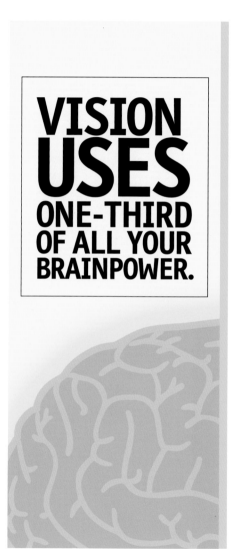

VISION USES ONE-THIRD OF ALL YOUR BRAINPOWER.

PARACHUTES WERE INVENTED BEFORE AIRPLANES.

An electric eel produces a charge strong enough to stun a horse.

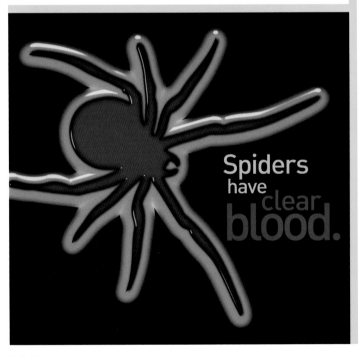

Spiders have clear blood.

SOME RATS CAN SURVIVE WITHOUT WATER LONGER THAN CAMELS.

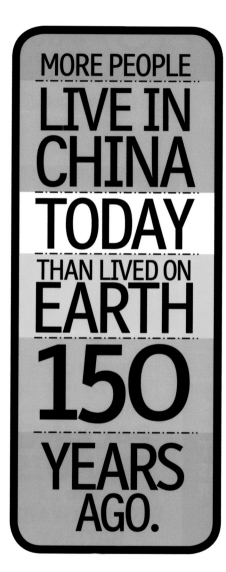

MORE PEOPLE LIVE IN CHINA TODAY THAN LIVED ON EARTH 150 YEARS AGO.

Ancient Egyptians believed that a person's **soul** was located in the **heart.**

Olympic gold medals are actually more than 90 percent **silver.**

Scientists call **EXOPLANETS** that orbit extremely close to their stars **"ROASTERS."**

In Great Britain, some people **EAT FRENCH TOAST WITH KETCHUP.**

A TRACTOR TRAILER SPILLED HUNDREDS of **FROZEN PIZZAS** across an Arkansas, U.S.A., interstate, causing a traffic jam.

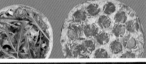

More than **8,000 PEOPLE** formed a **GIANT SMILEY FACE** in a park in Manila, Philippines.

Sir Isaac Newton tried for years to **TURN LEAD INTO GOLD.**

THOUSANDS of **SEA SALPS** (small jellyfish-like creatures) can combine to form **15-FOOT** (4.6-m)-**LONG CHAINS UNDERWATER** as they hunt.

Researchers have figured out how to turn **PACKING PEANUTS** into **RECHARGEABLE BATTERY COMPONENTS.**

A STUDY FOUND that PEOPLE like a **ROBOT** better when it makes **A FEW MISTAKES.**

LIZARD MAN
=
a scaly **SEVEN-FOOT-** (2-m) **TALL** version of **BIGFOOT** local to South Carolina, U.S.A.

In *The Oxford English Dictionary,* the word **"SET"** has a definition that's **60,000** words long.

The U.S. Postal Service **DELIVERS MAIL BY HOVERCRAFT.**

That's Weird!

A GIANT TORTOISE named **ABUH** escaped from a zoo in Japan twice in two weeks.

A gingerbread house was once decorated with **4,750** pounds (2,155 kg) of icing—that's heavier than a **giraffe.**

IS THERE A RECORD FOR THE CUTEST HOUSE?

ASTRONAUTS' FOOTPRINTS STAY ON THE MOON FOREVER; THERE'S NO WIND TO BLOW THEM AWAY.

New Zealand HAS MORE sheep THAN people.

Giant TORTOISES KEEP GROWING FOR THEIR WHOLE LIVES.

MORE THAN
10 MILLION
MILLIONAIRES
ARE ALIVE
TODAY.

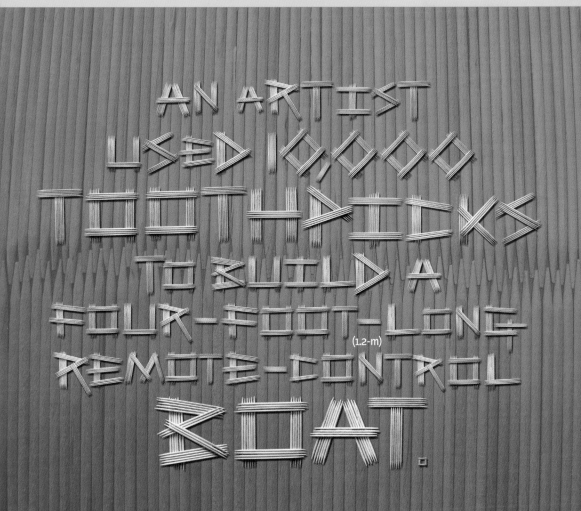

AN ARTIST USED 10,000 TOOTHPICKS TO BUILD A FOUR-FOOT-LONG (1.2-m) REMOTE-CONTROL BOAT.

EARTHWORMS HAVE 5 HEARTS.

Ladybugs squirt smelly liquid from their knees when they *get scared.*

IF YOU *RUN* IN THE RAIN, YOU WILL GET ABOUT **50%** WETTER THAN IF YOU STAND STILL.

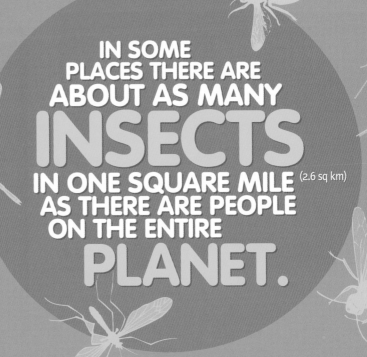

IN SOME
PLACES THERE ARE
ABOUT AS MANY
INSECTS
IN ONE SQUARE MILE (2.6 sq km)
AS THERE ARE PEOPLE
ON THE ENTIRE
PLANET.

HONEYBEES CAN BE TRAINED TO DETECT EXPLOSIVES.

Traffic lights were invented

before

CARS.

THERE ARE MORE STARS IN THE UNIVERSE THAN GRAINS OF SAND ON EARTH.

THE LONGEST MONOPOLY GAME PLAYED IN A BATHTUB LASTED

99

HOURS.

Blue whales ARE THE largest animals THAT EVER lived—THEY'RE EVEN BIGGER THAN dinosaurs!

CLEOPATRA BECAME THE QUEEN OF EGYPT WHEN SHE WAS ONLY A TEENAGER.

Panda droppings can be made into paper.

The largest **dinosaurs** were vegetarians.

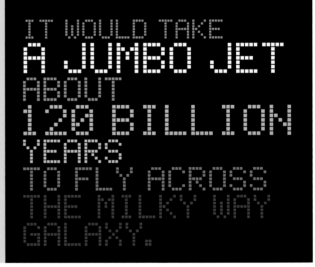

IT WOULD TAKE A JUMBO JET ABOUT 120 BILLION YEARS TO FLY ACROSS THE MILKY WAY GALAXY.

A **pet** goldfish in England lived to be **43** years old.

RED RAIN HAS FALLEN IN PARTS OF EUROPE AND ASIA.

Catnip can affect lions and tigers.

A HURRICANE ON JUPITER IS MORE THAN 300 YEARS OLD AND STILL GOING STRONG!

THE
WORLD'S
HEAVIEST
ONION
WEIGHED
MORE
THAN A MAN'S
HEAD.

In Peru it's considered good luck to wear yellow underwear on New Year's Day.

SKIN
IS
YOUR
BODY'S
LARGEST
ORGAN.

THE
ANCIENT
EGYPTIANS
TRAINED
MONKEYS
TO
DANCE
AND
PLAY MUSIC.

Mike the
chicken
lived for
18
months
without
a head,
from 1945 to
1947.

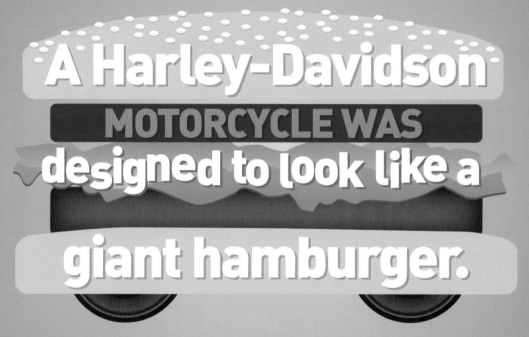

A Harley-Davidson MOTORCYCLE WAS designed to look like a giant hamburger.

Chimpanzees, monkeys, dogs, mice, and a guinea pig have all journeyed into space.

One of the largest man-made islands is shaped like a palm tree.

You can buy **a diamond dog collar** for about **$3 million.**

A MAN WAS STRUCK BY LIGHTNING **7** TIMES AND LIVED!

147

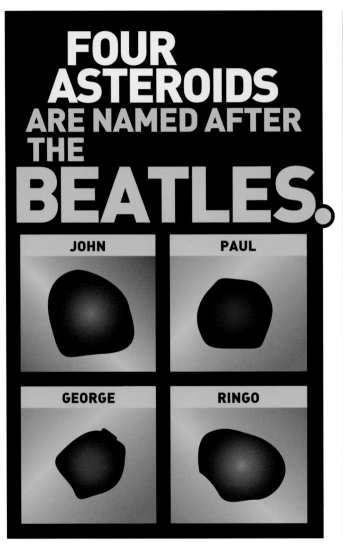

FOUR ASTEROIDS ARE NAMED AFTER THE BEATLES.

JOHN	PAUL
GEORGE	RINGO

If you fell into a black hole, you'd stretch out like s p a g h e t t i.

Crickets detect sound through their knees.

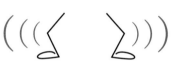

THERE IS CELL PHONE RECEPTION AT THE SUMMIT OF MOUNT EVEREST.

SOME **wild** turkeys run UP TO **25** miles an hour. (40 km/h)

A BAKING COMPANY CREATED A CHOCOLATE CHIP COOKIE THAT WEIGHED AS MUCH AS SEVEN PICKUP TRUCKS.

A COMET is a gigantic ball of dirt and ice.

The **smallest monkey** is about as tall as a **toothbrush.**

A
GRIZZLY
BEAR
CAN RUN
AS FAST
AS A
HORSE.

Astronauts have grown potatoes on the space shuttle.

A man

once rode

a bike

down the

Eiffel

Tower's

1,665

steps.

The holes in
Swiss
cheese
**are called
eyes.**

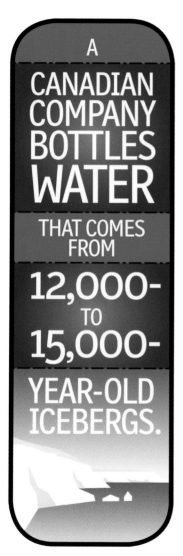

A CANADIAN COMPANY BOTTLES **WATER** THAT COMES FROM **12,000-** TO **15,000-** YEAR-OLD ICEBERGS.

A HIGHWAY RUNS THROUGH THE MIDDLE OF AN OFFICE BUILDING IN OSAKA, JAPAN.

THE WORLD'S MOST EXPENSIVE TREE HOUSE, LOCATED IN THE UNITED KINGDOM, COST £3.7 MILLION TO BUILD.

A GREAT WHITE SHARK CAN WEIGH AS MUCH AS 15 GORILLAS.

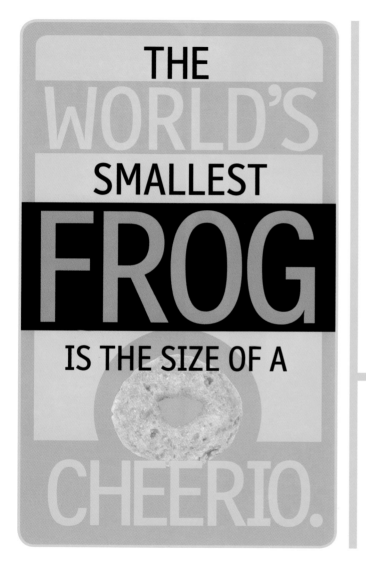

THE
WORLD'S
SMALLEST
FROG
IS THE SIZE OF A
CHEERIO.

A pizza topped with **24-karat gold** sold for more than **$4,000.**

The world's **termites outweigh** the world's **people.**

159

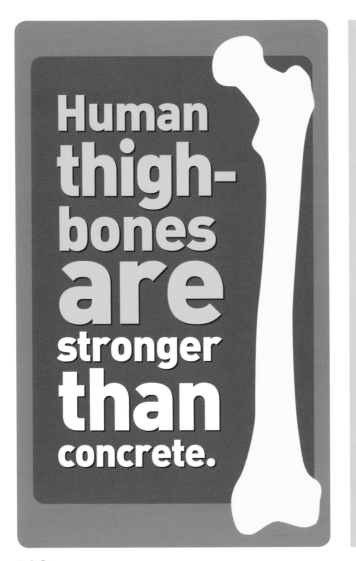

Human thigh-bones are stronger than concrete.

THE PLANET EARTH ROTATES 1.5 MILLISECONDS SLOWER EVERY CENTURY.

Snowflakes get smaller as the **TEMPERATURE DROPS.**

A
JELLYFISH
CAN BE AS
SMALL
AS A
THIMBLE
OR AS
LARGE
AS
TWO
WASHING
MACHINES.

FISHERMEN in Tanzania **USE SPIDER SILK** as fishing line.

The **MEXICAN MOLE LIZARD** has only **TWO LEGS.**

The **STATE VEGETABLE** OF VERMONT, U.S.A., is the **GILFEATHER TURNIP.**

A variety of **KALE** called the **JERSEY WALKING STICK** can grow more than **13** feet tall. (4 m)

SCIENTISTS DETECTED **RADIO SIGNALS FROM A DWARF STAR** 11 light-years from Earth.

In Guangzhou, China, **1,069** ROBOTS showed off their moves during a **SYNCHRONIZED DANCE PARTY.**

TWO CATS in **Thailand** were once **"MARRIED"** in a CEREMONY that COST MORE THAN **$16,000.**

BABY WILDEBEEST know to **FOLLOW THEIR HERD WITHIN ONE HOUR** of being born.

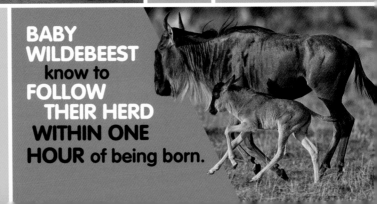

In an **AVERAGE BASEBALL GAME,** more than an hour total is spent **waiting around between pitches,** a study found.

Twillionaire = a person with more than a million Twitter followers

A food truck in Portland, Oregon, U.S.A., SERVES A **HAZELNUT BUTTER, JAM, AND DUCK SANDWICH.**

That's Weird! ••

There's a **WEBSITE** that **"TRANSLATES" WORDS** INTO ELEPHANT-SPEAK.

CHIMPANZEES can learn to play **ROCK-PAPER-SCISSORS.**

A STACK OF A BILLION DOLLAR BILLS WEIGHS MORE THAN 15 ARMY TANKS.

A **newborn kangaroo** is about as long as a **paper clip.**

Giant anteaters can

A BABY PORCUPINE IS CALLED A PORCUPETTE.

A peanut is not a nut.

THE **FIRST** TELEPHONE ANSWERING MACHINE WAS

3

FEET TALL.
(0.9 m)

eat more than 30,000 insects in a day.

There are
31,556,926
seconds
in a year.

THE BIGGEST INHABITED PALACE ON EARTH

(IN THE SOUTHEAST ASIAN COUNTRY OF BRUNEI)

HAS

1,788 ROOMS.

A CLOUD CAN WEIGH MORE THAN A MILLION POUNDS.
(453,593 kg)

The Amazon rain forest is home to giant rodents— called capybaras— that are about as tall as German shepherds.

The Chihuahua is the world's smallest dog breed.

Birds
are
descended from
dinosaurs.

MARSHMALLOWS
WERE ORIGINALLY
MADE FROM
ROOTS OF A PLANT
CALLED THE
MARSH-
MALLOW.

20%
of the food
we eat
is used to
fuel
THE
BRAIN.

EVERY DAY IS ABOUT 55 BILLIONTHS OF A SECOND LONGER THAN THE DAY BEFORE IT.

The skin of a golden poison dart frog contains enough toxins to kill up to **100 people.**

Gorillas **burp** when they're **happy.**

HUMMINGBIRDS are the only birds that can fly **BACKWARD.**

ABOUT ONE-QUARTER OF THE

body's bones are
in the feet —that's 52 out of more than 200!

A SPACE SUIT WEIGHS 280 POUNDS— (127 kg) WITHOUT AN ASTRONAUT IN IT.

Elephants sometimes make **purr-like** sounds when content.

Baby
RATTLESNAKES
are born without
RATTLES.

The Milky Way is made up of at least **100** billion stars.

SOME SAND DUNES *BARK*.

You use **72** different muscles every time you talk.

Your body
contains about
60,000
miles
(96,561 km)

of blood
vessels.

Strawberries have more VITAMIN C than oranges.

Palm trees grew at the **North Pole** about 55 million years ago.

A SNAIL
WOULD TAKE ABOUT **220 HOURS TO CRAWL ONE MILE** (1.6 km) **NONSTOP.**

The **Basenji,** **a dog from Africa,** **yodels** instead of **barking.**

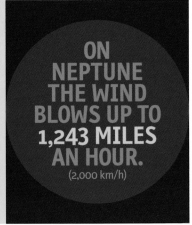

ON NEPTUNE THE WIND BLOWS UP TO **1,243 MILES AN HOUR.** (2,000 km/h)

"HAPPY BIRTHDAY" WAS THE FIRST SONG TRANSMITTED FROM SPACE TO EARTH.

THE WORLD'S LONGEST
mountain range
is under the
sea.

An average adult's
skin.
weighs about 11 pounds.
(5 kg)

IF YOU EAT TOO MANY CARROTS, YOUR SKIN CAN TURN ORANGE.

189

A CROCODILE CAN'T STICK ITS TONGUE OUT.

THE NUMBER OF TIMES **some crickets chirp** each second **can be used to estimate** the **temperature.**

You lose about **NINE POUNDS** of skin cells every year.

(4.1 kg)

You can't move your body when you're **dreaming.**

ARACHIBUTYROPHOBIA IS THE **FEAR** OF GETTING PEANUT BUTTER STUCK TO THE ROOF OF YOUR **MOUTH.**

The
face in the
"Mona Lisa"
has no
eye-
brOws.

You're almost a half inch taller (1.3 cm) in the morning than in the evening.

Astronauts can't whistle ON THE MOON.

Death Valley, California, U.S.A., IS THE hottest PLACE IN North America.

Human ears evolved from ancient **FISH GILLS.**

THAT'S WEIRD!

THE LONGEST RECORDED
FLIGHT OF A

ALL OF THE BLOOD IN YOUR BODY TRAVELS THROUGH YOUR HEART ONCE A MINUTE.

IT'S IMPOSSIBLE TO BREATHE AND SWALLOW AT THE SAME TIME.

*CHICKEN IS **13** SECONDS.*

THE OLDEST HUMAN FOOTPRINT EVER FOUND IS 350,000 YEARS OLD.

A 100-POUND PERSON (45-kg) WOULD WEIGH 38 POUNDS (17 kg) ON MARS.

Your *hair* **grows faster** IN **WARM WEATHER.**

THE MALE KILLER WHALE'S DORSAL (BACK) FIN IS ALMOST SIX FEET (1.8 m) **HIGH— THE HEIGHT OF A TALL MAN.**

A **LIZARD-LIKE REPTILE CALLED A TUATARA HAS A** **THIRD EYE** ON TOP OF ITS **HEAD.**

THE YEAR
2020
is the next time you can see a full moon on Halloween.

GHOST BATS are some of the only bats with WHITE FUR.

Sharks have **eight** senses.

A **coyote** can hear a mouse moving **under** a **foot of snow.**

(0.3 m)

Humans have only five.

The **human** **body** contains enough **iron** to make a **two-inch** **nail.**
(5.1-cm)

CROCODILES HAVE BEEN AROUND FOR ABOUT **200** MILLION YEARS.

MOUNTAIN LIONS CAN WHISTLE.

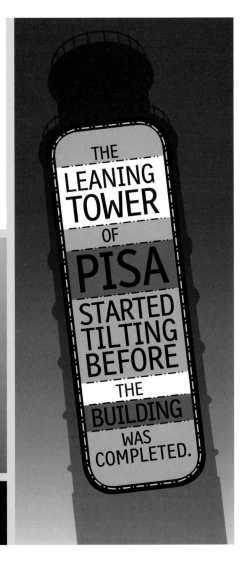

THE LEANING TOWER OF PISA STARTED TILTING BEFORE THE BUILDING WAS COMPLETED.

It's **impossible** for a person to **sink** in the **Dead Sea.**

Your **heart** is about the same size as your **fist.**

THE HORNED DINOSAUR *DRACOREX HOGWARTSIA* WAS NAMED AFTER **HOGWARTS,** HARRY POTTER'S SCHOOL.

MORE WATER IS IN THE PACIFIC OCEAN THAN IN ALL OF THE OTHER SEAS AND OCEANS COMBINED.

206

99% of people can't lick their elbows.

THAT'S REALLY WEIRD!

(But 90% of people who read this will try!)

GUESS WHAT?

Some dogs don't wag their tails!

WHY?

Your brain is smaller than a _____'s brain!

WHAT?

Scientists know more about this place in space than this place on Earth!

WHERE?

WANNA FIND OUT?

The FUN doesn't have to end here! Find these far-out facts and more in *Weird But True! 2*.

NATIONAL GEOGRAPHIC KiDS

FACTFINDER

Boldface indicates illustrations.

FACTFINDER

FACTFINDER

213

FACTFINDER

PHOTOCREDITS

Published by National Geographic Partners, LLC.
All rights reserved. Reproduction of the whole
or any part of the contents without written
permission from the publisher is prohibited.

Since 1888, the National Geographic Society has
funded more than 12,000 research, exploration,
and preservation projects around the world.
The Society receives funds from National
Geographic Partners, LLC, funded in part by
your purchase. A portion of the proceeds from
this book supports this vital work. To learn
more, visit natgeo.com/info.

NATIONAL GEOGRAPHIC and Yellow Border
Design are trademarks of the National
Geographic Society, used under license.

For more information, visit
nationalgeographic.com, call 1-800-647-5463,
or write to the following address:

National Geographic Partners
1145 17th Street N.W.
Washington, D.C. 20036-4688 U.S.A.

Visit us online at nationalgeographic.com/books

For librarians and teachers:
ngchildrensbooks.org

More for kids from National Geographic:
natgeokids.com

For information about special discounts
for bulk purchases, please contact National
Geographic Books Special Sales:
specialsales@natgeo.com

For rights or permissions inquiries, please
contact National Geographic Books Subsidiary
Rights: bookrights@natgeo.com

Designed by Rachael Hamm Plett, Moduza Design

First edition published 2010
Reissued and updated 2018

Trade paperback: 978-1-4263-3104-6
Reinforced library binding ISBN:
978-1-4263-3105-3

The publisher would like to thank Jen Agresta,
project manager; Julie Beer, researcher;
Jo Tunstall, researcher; Robin Terry, project
editor; Paige Towler, project editor; Eva
Absher-Schantz, art director; Julide Dengel,
art director; Kathryn Robbins, art director;
Ruthie Thompson, designer; Lori Epstein, photo
director; Hillary Leo, photo editor; and Anne
LeongSon and Gus Tello, production assistants.

Printed in China
18/PPS/1